By Author: Joseph Sumpter

Book Title: Relaxing Activity For Adults: Wonderful Dogs and Puppies Coloring Book For Adults Relaxation and Stress Relief

Cute dogs and puppies that adults would enjoy coloring for fun activity, relaxation, and stress relief.

Biography

Joseph Sumpter enjoys creating books, traveling, sports, and working.

Copyright 2015

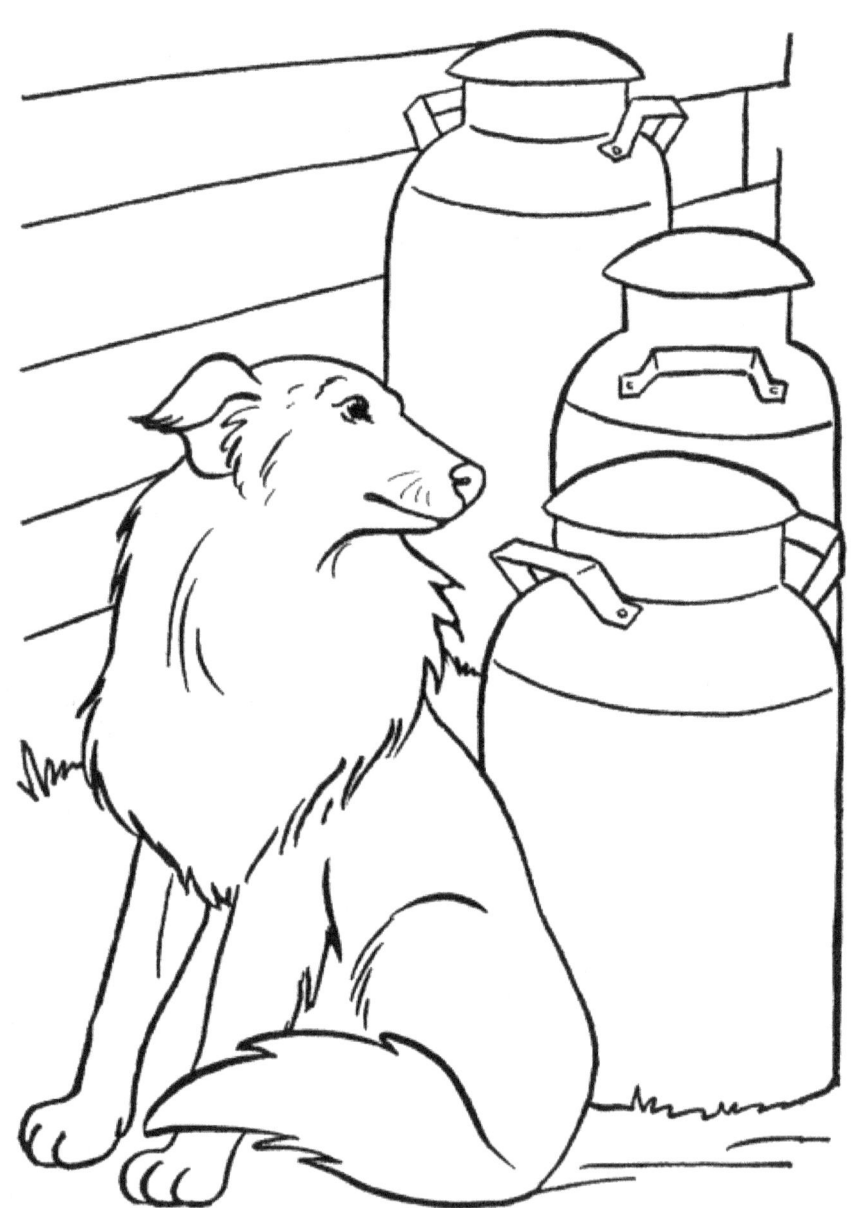

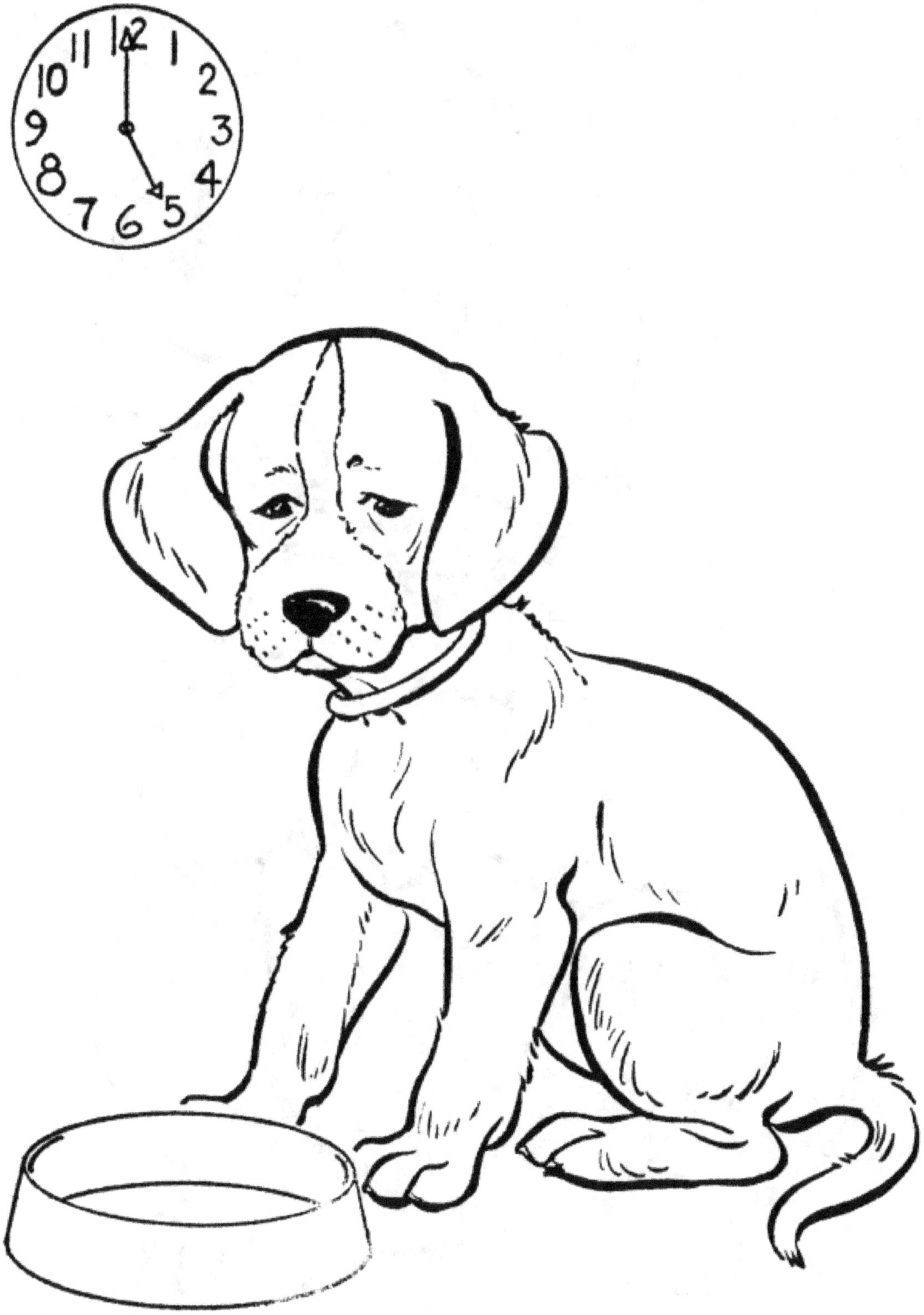

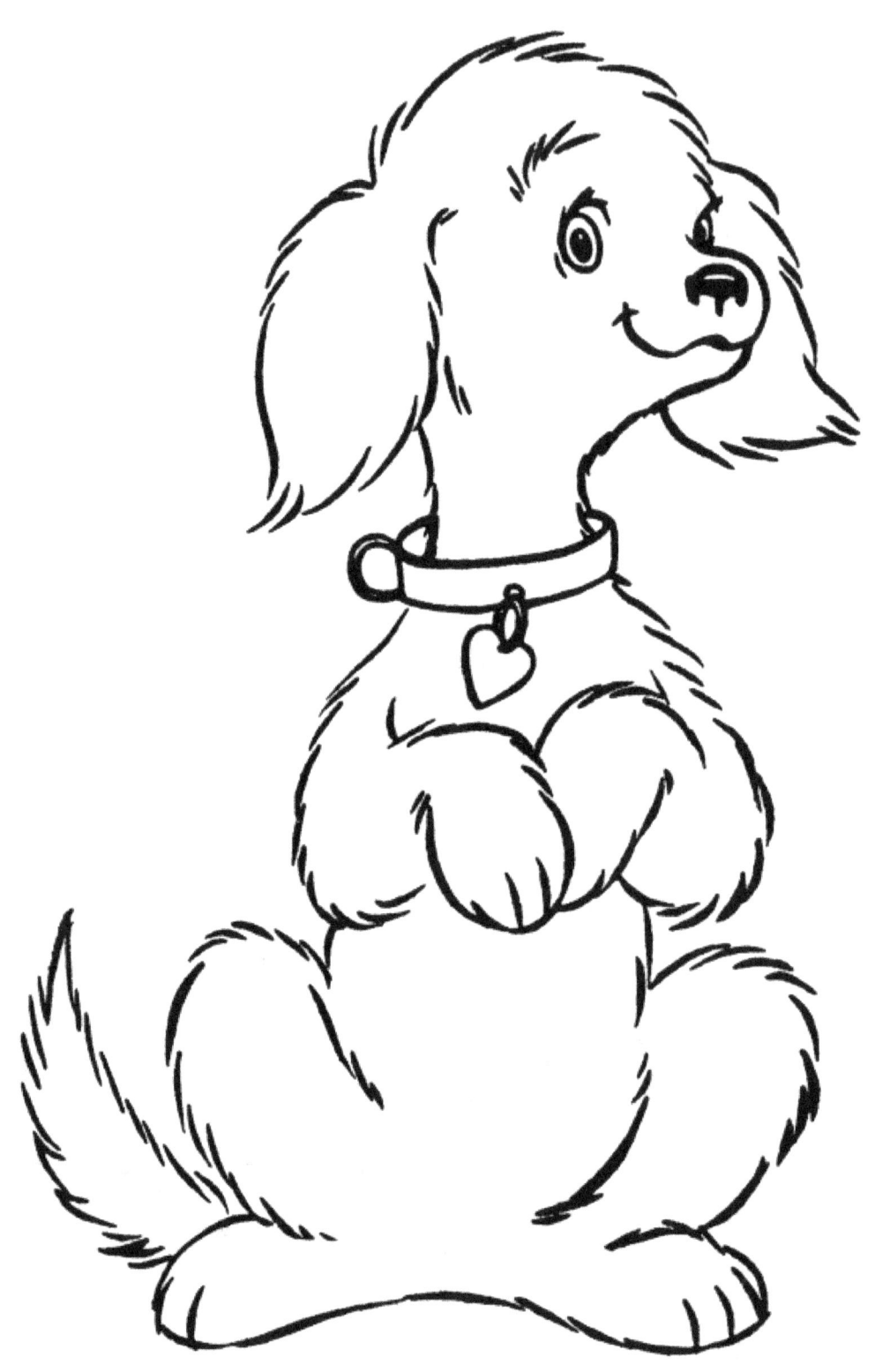

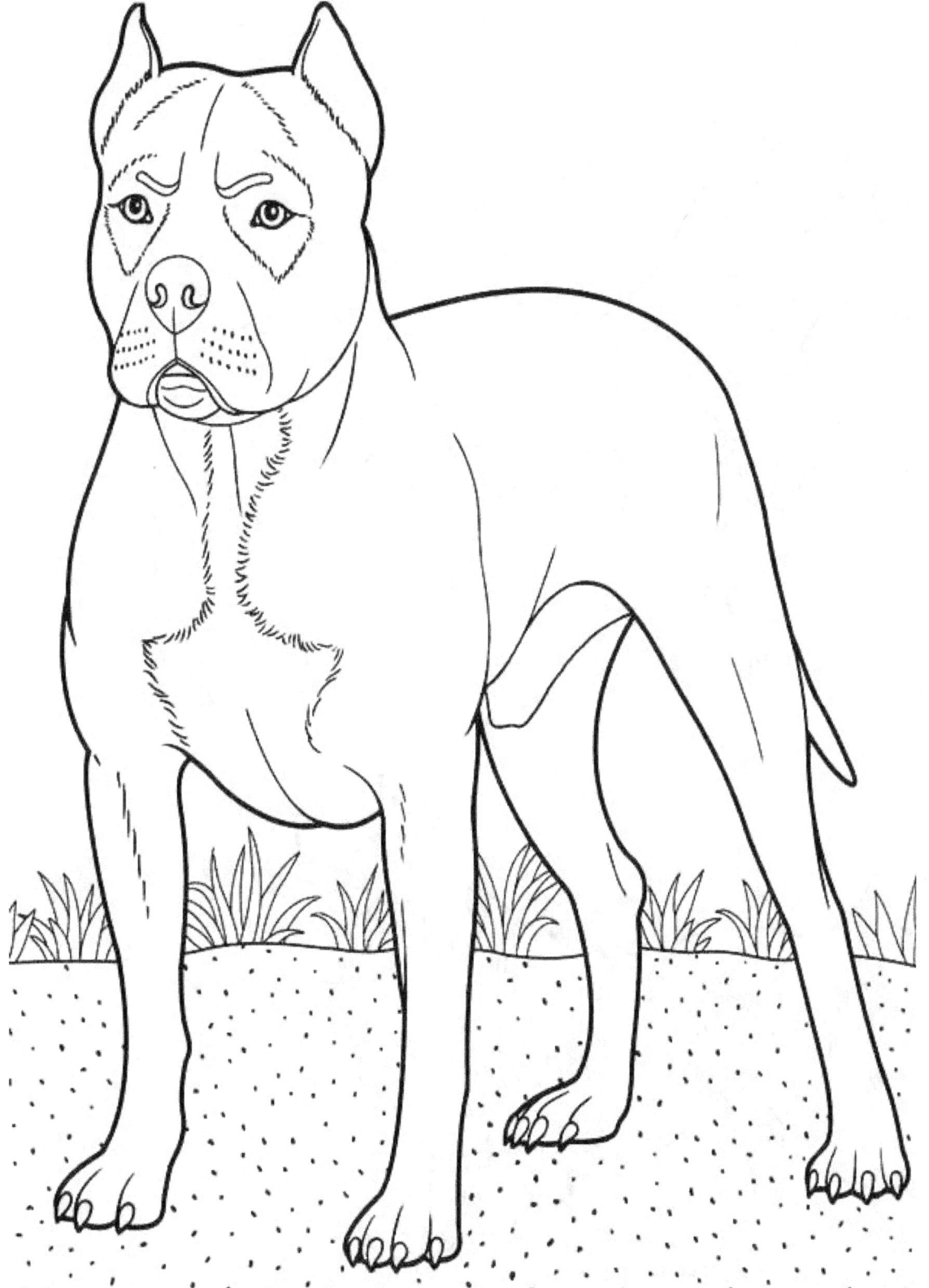

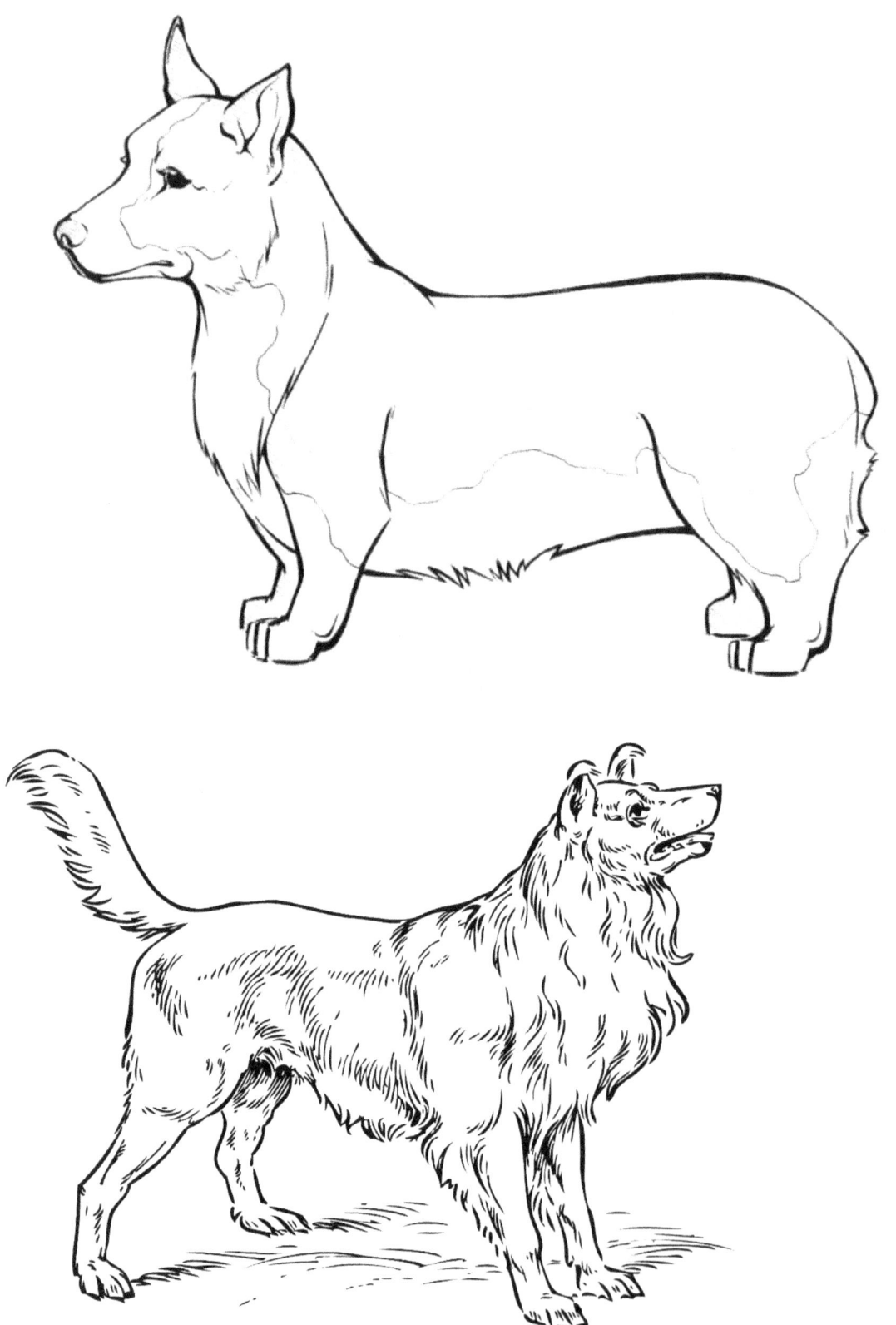

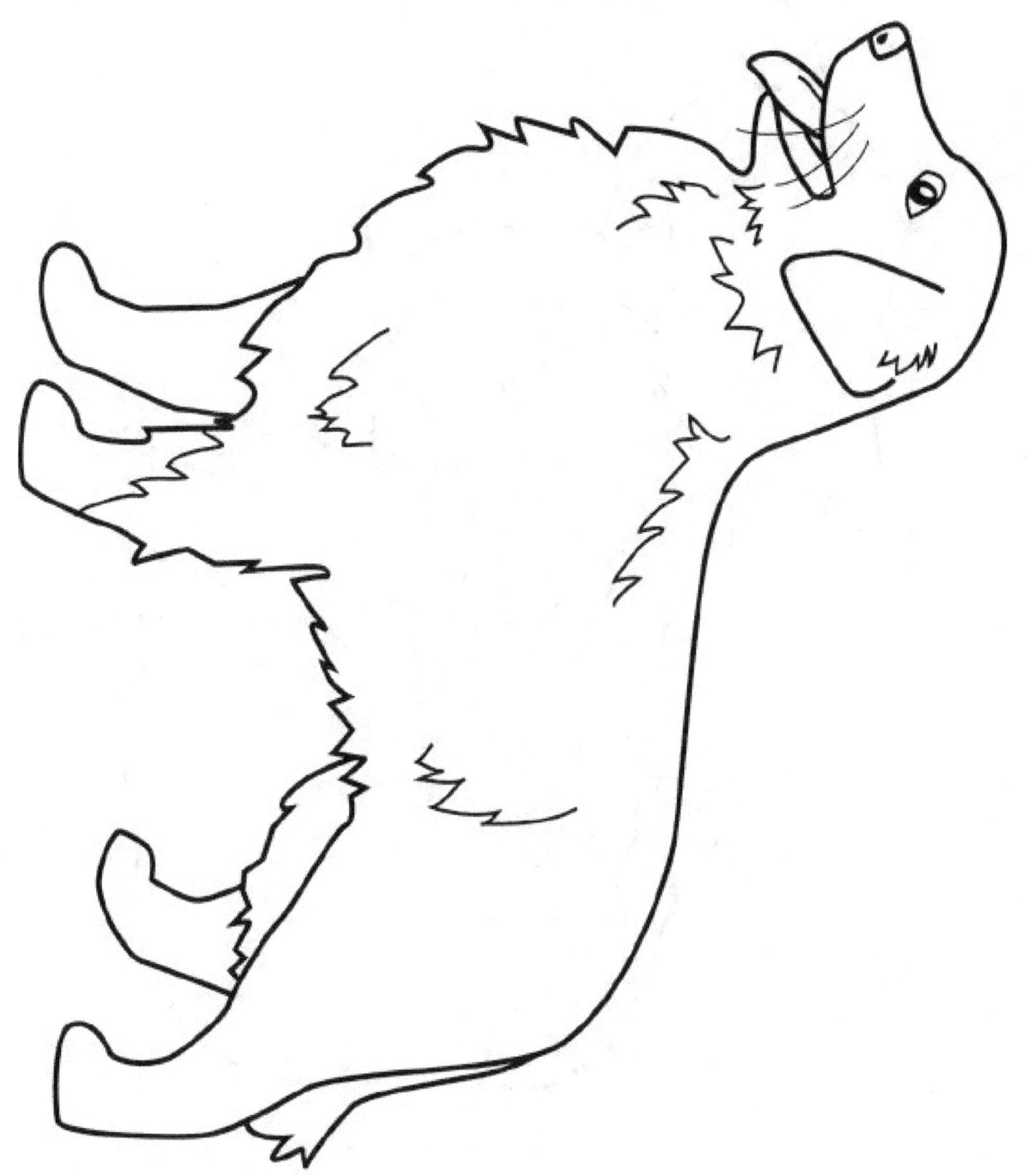

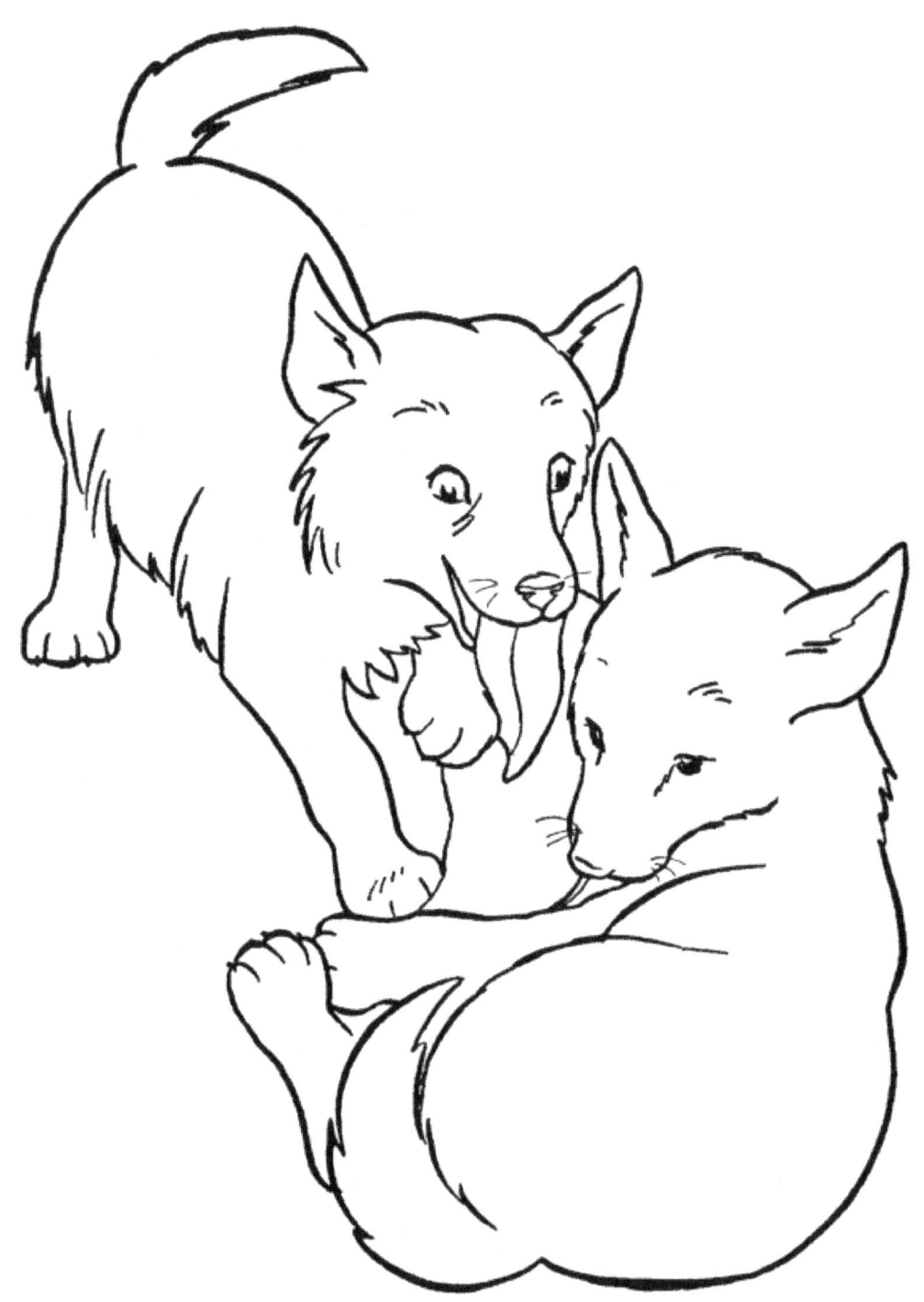

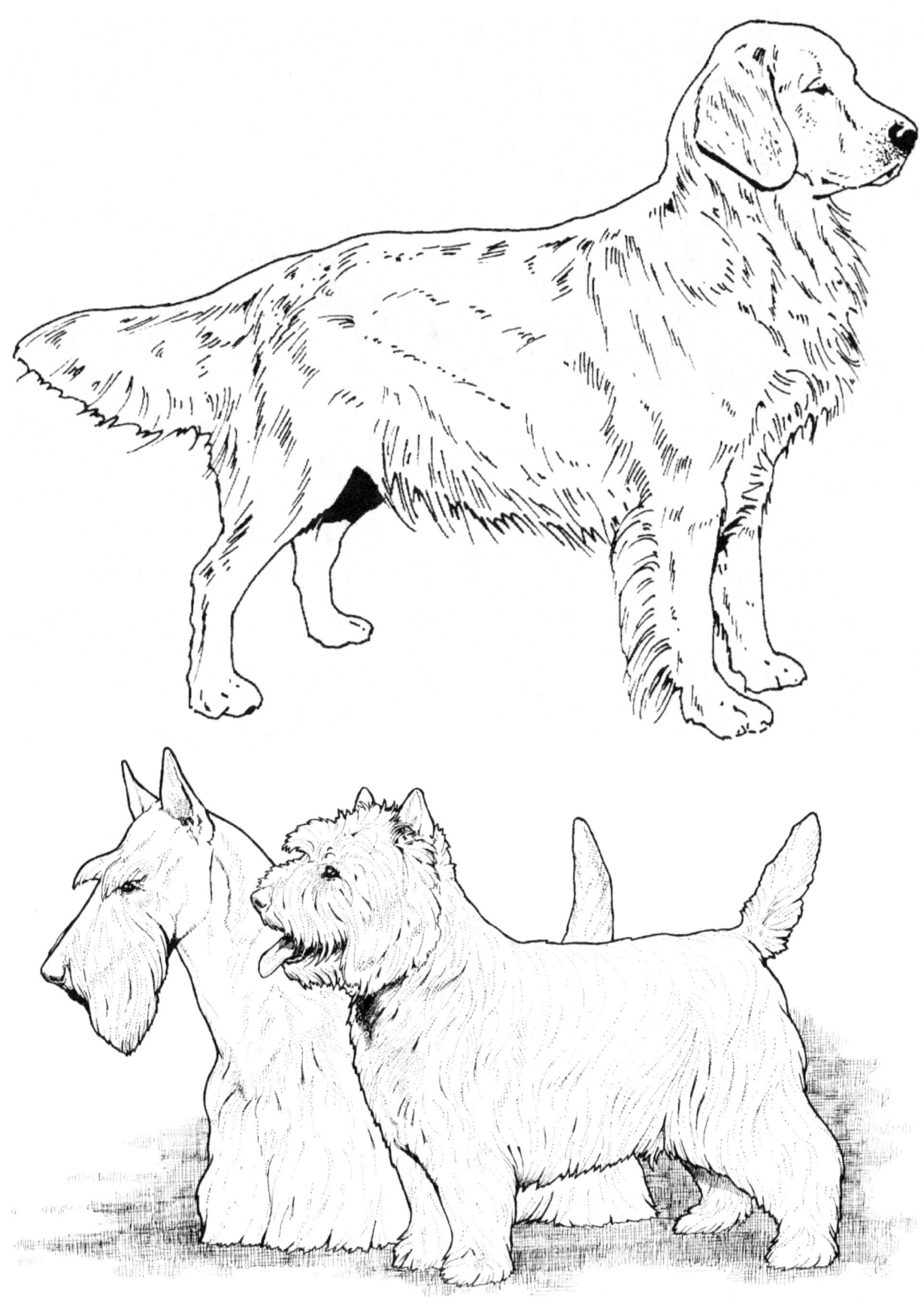

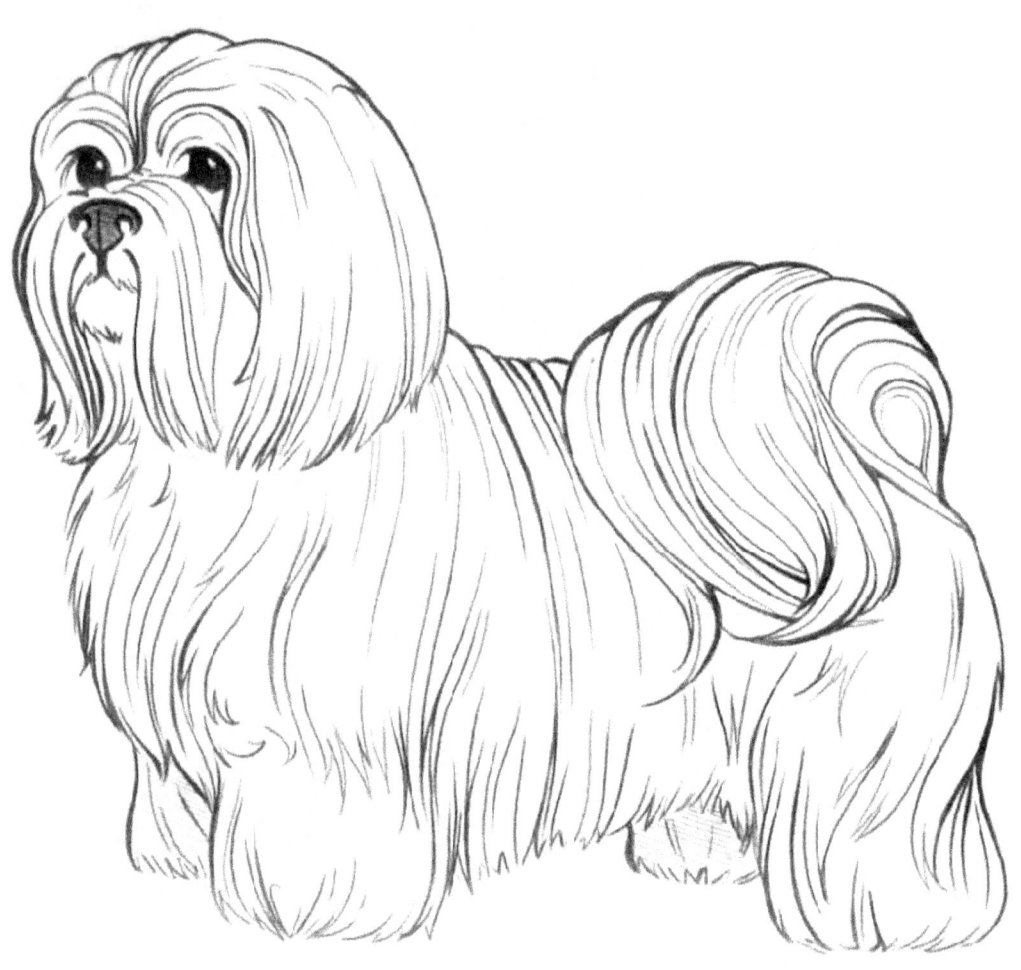

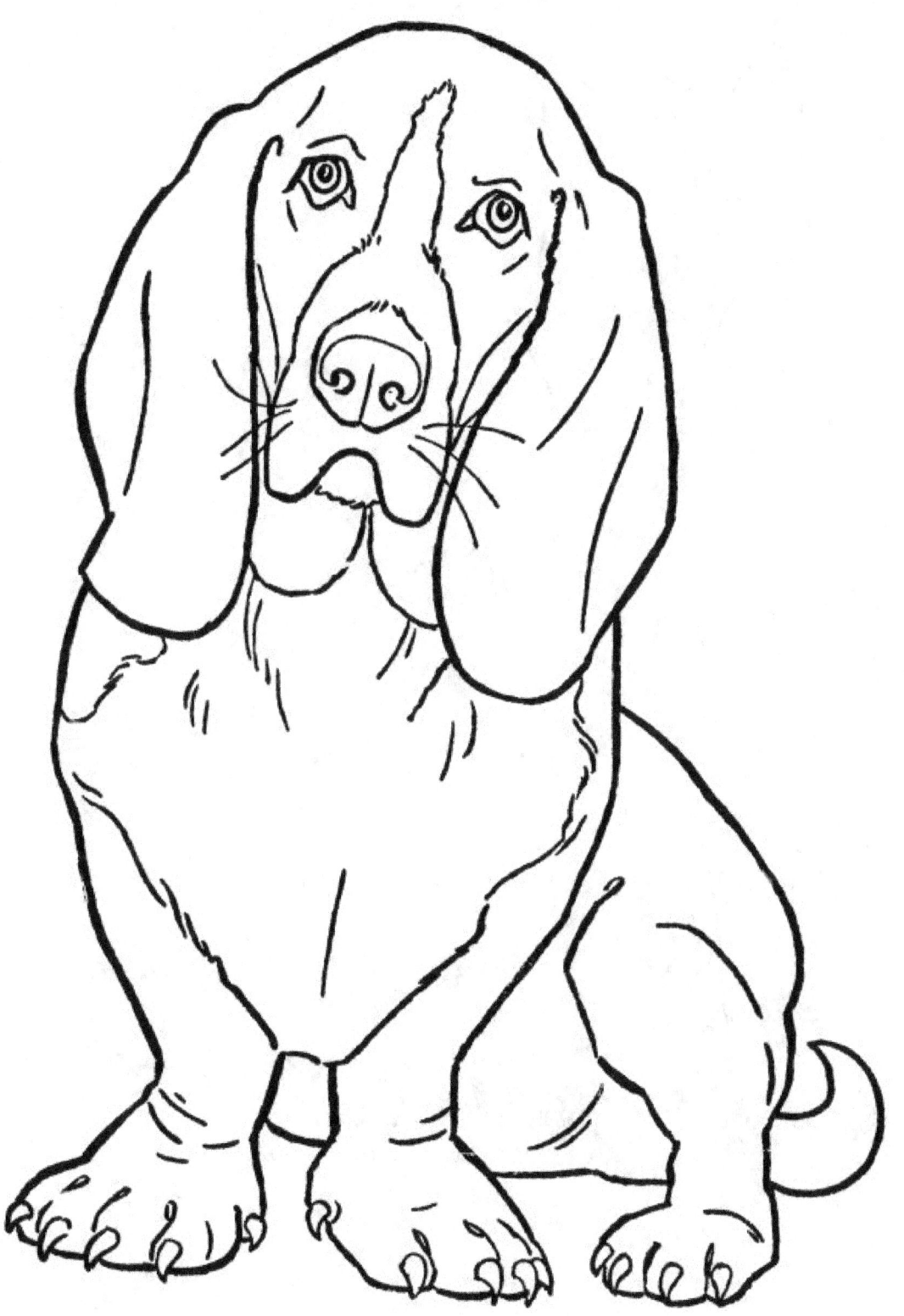

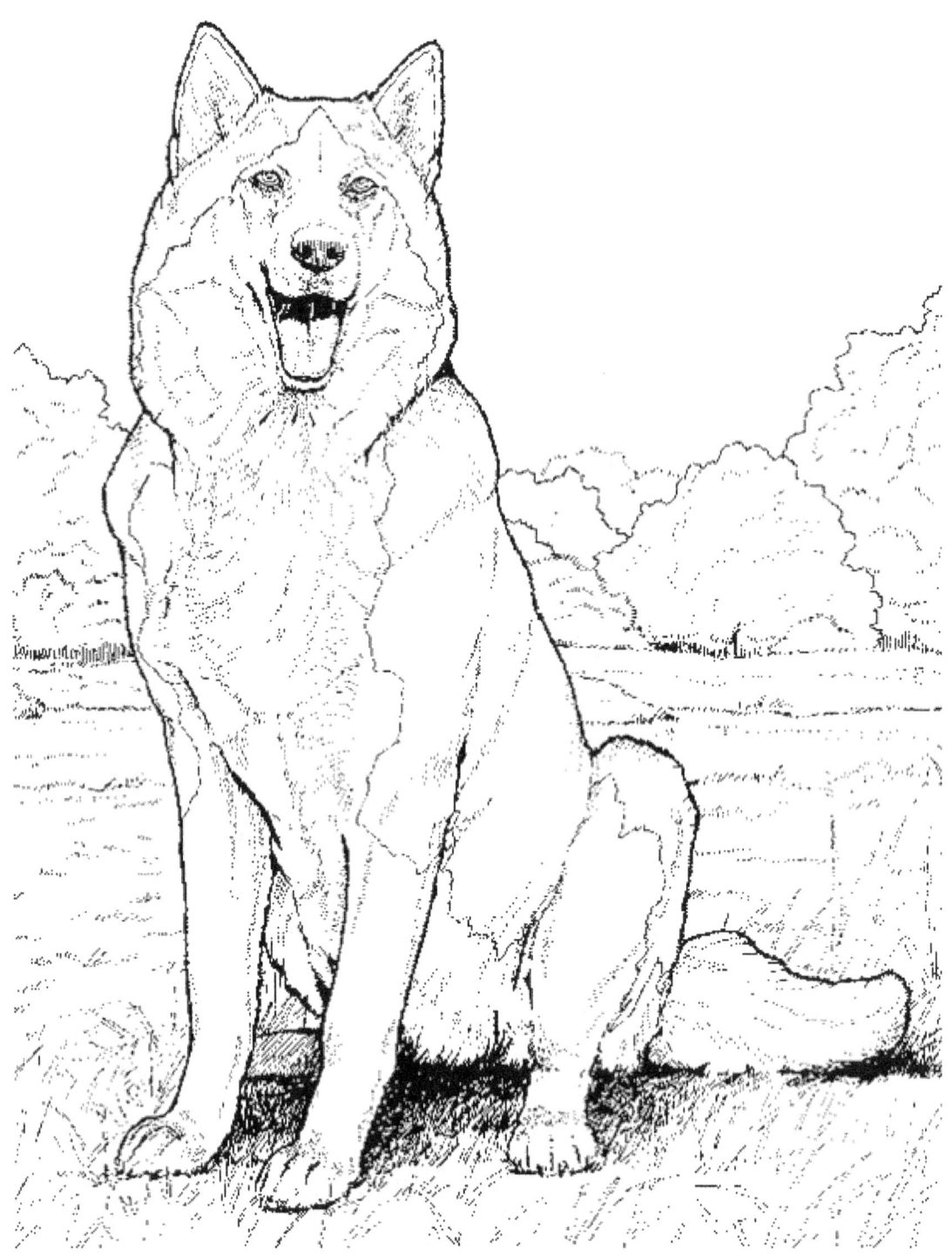

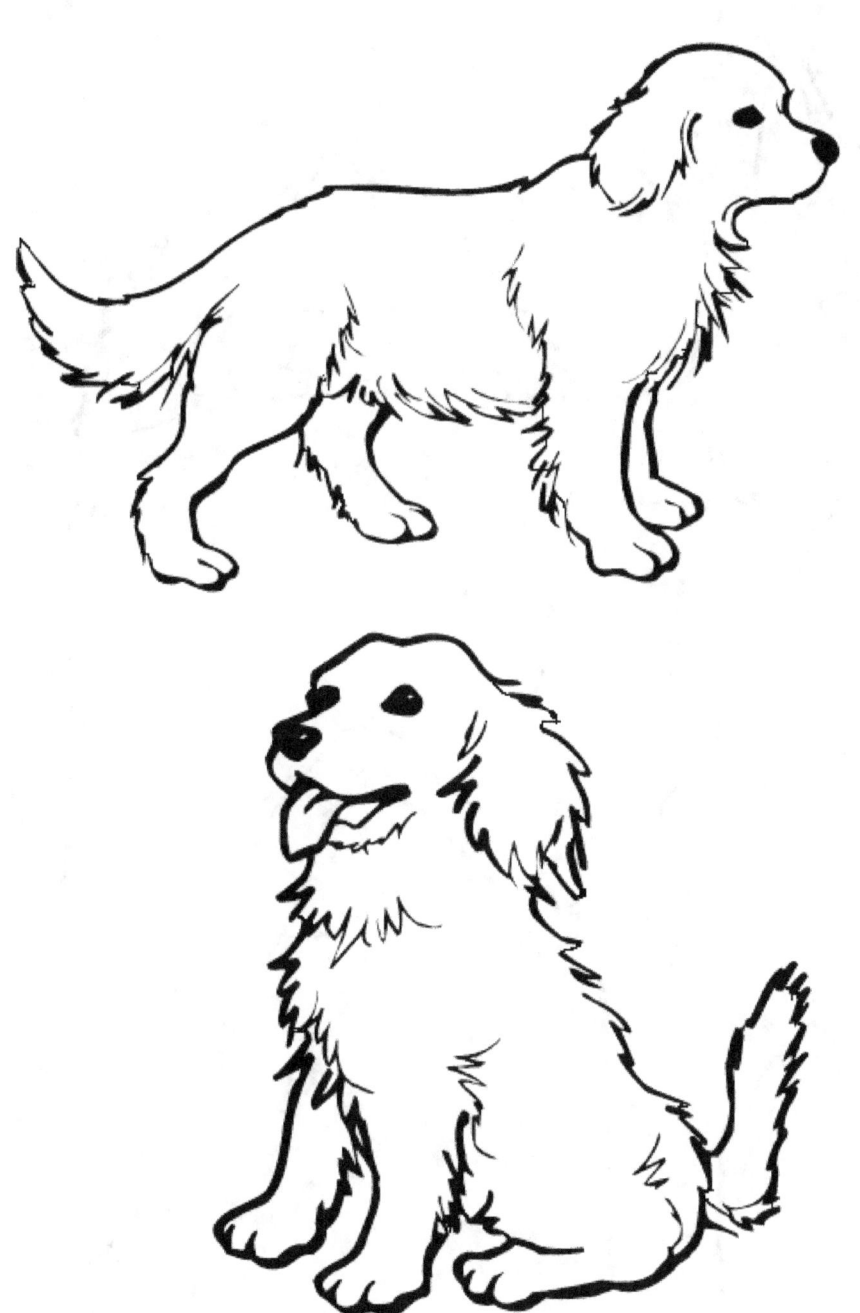

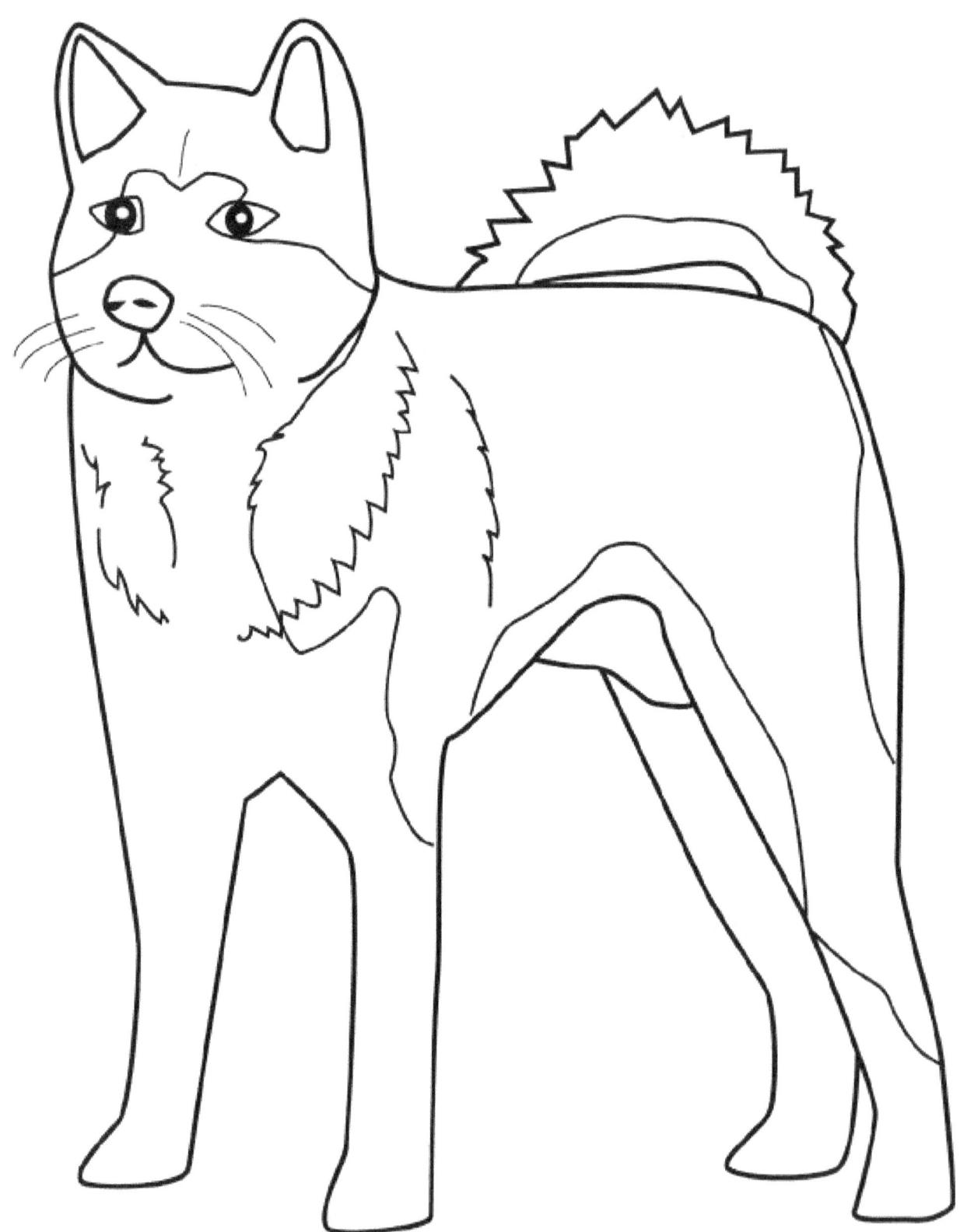

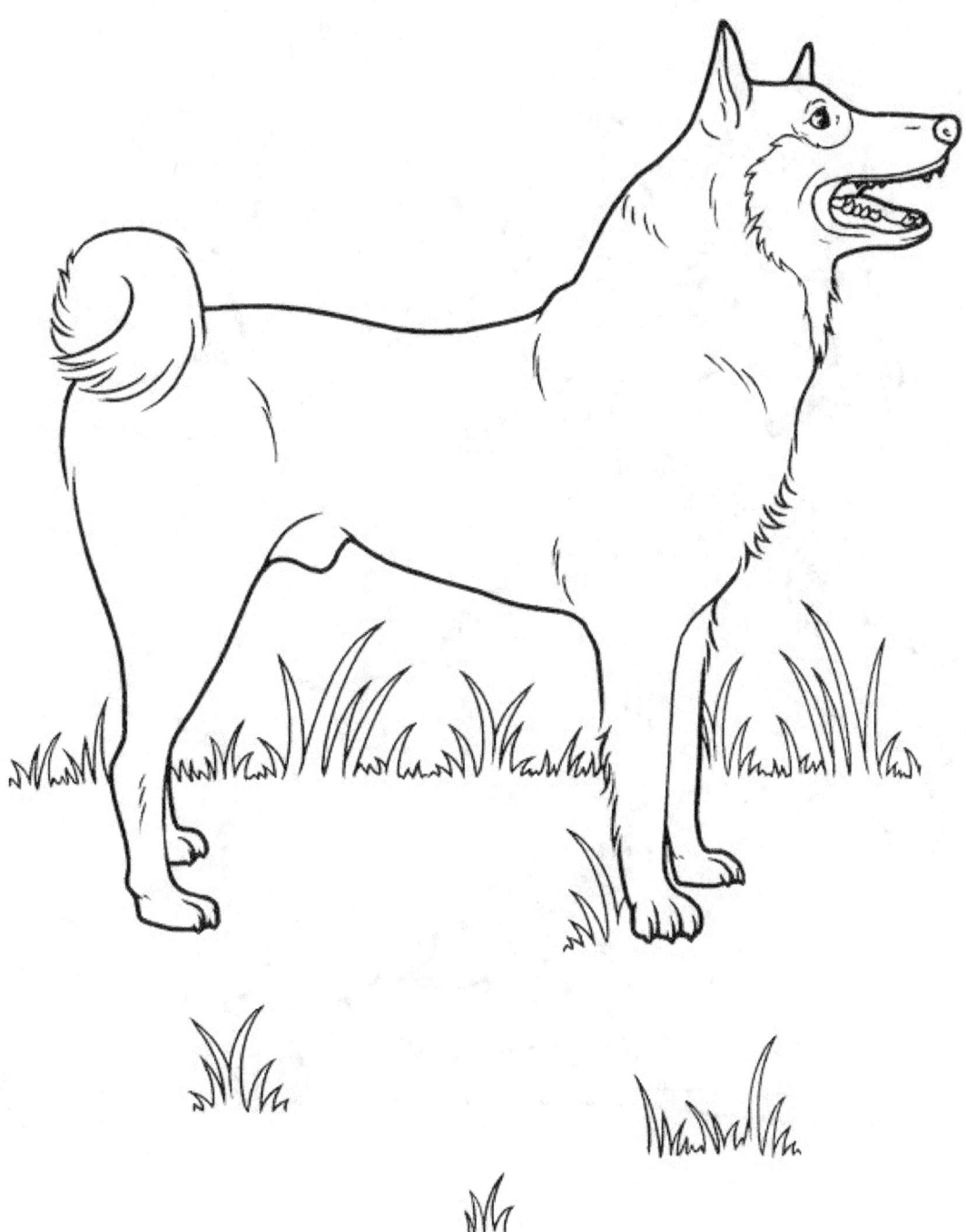

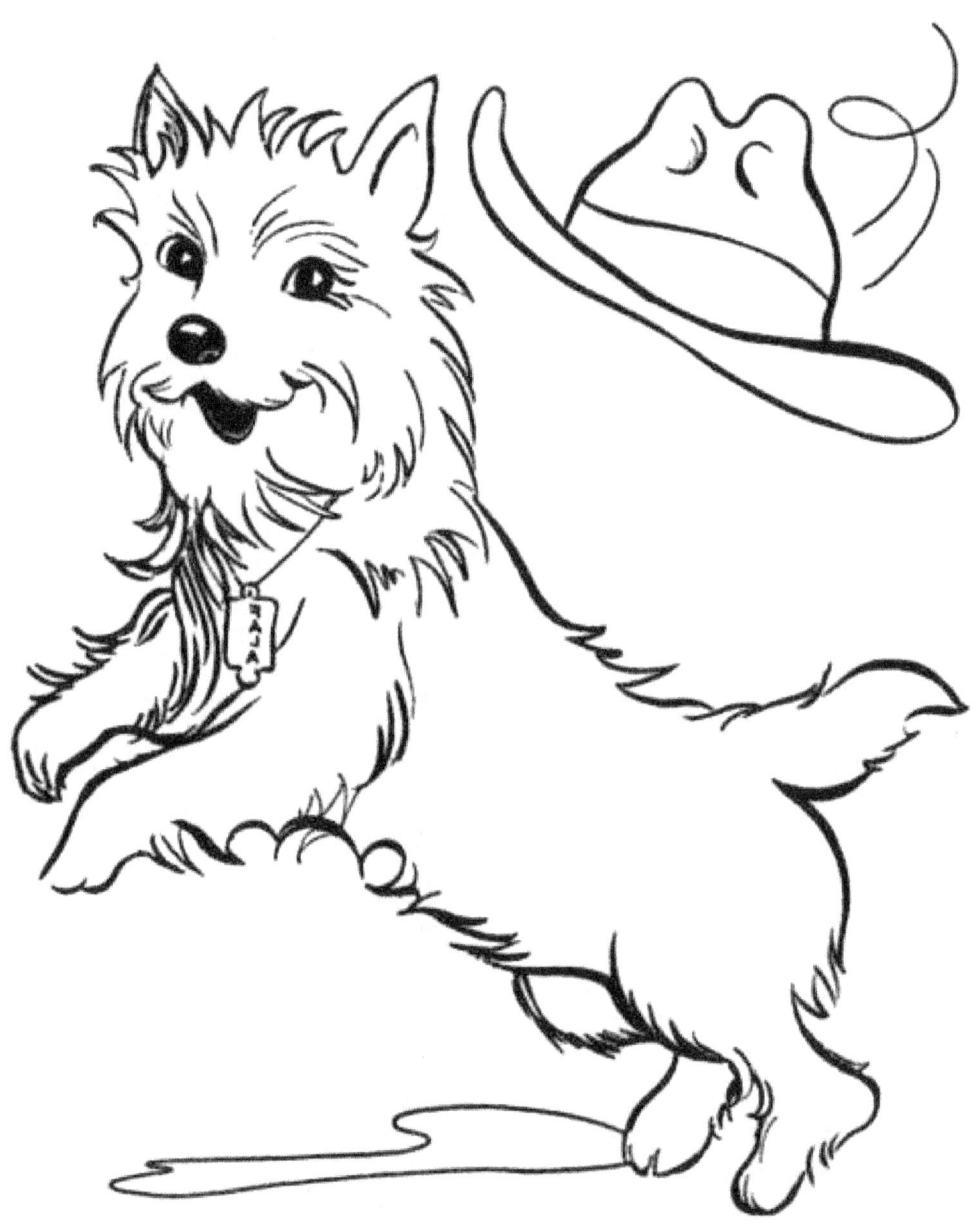

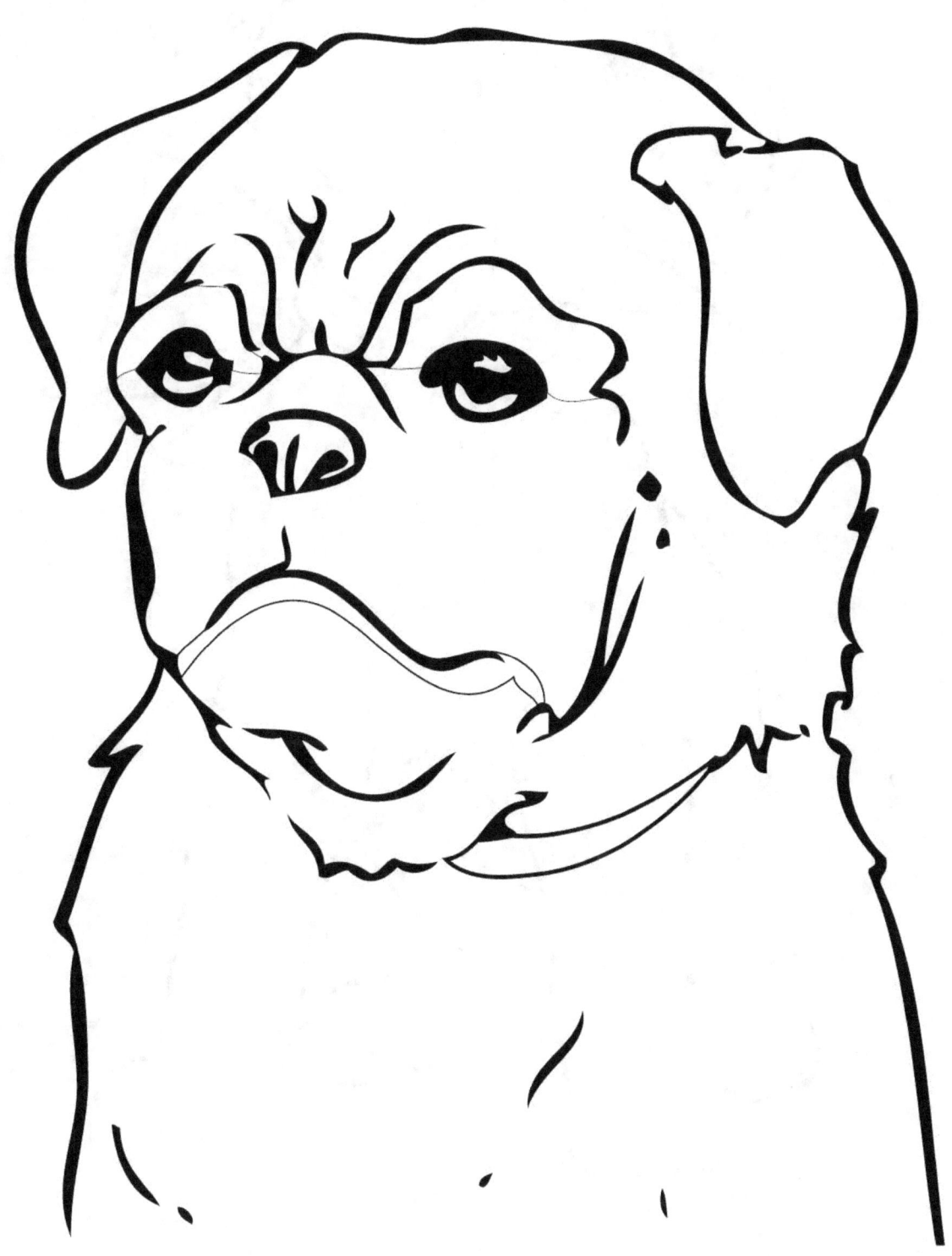

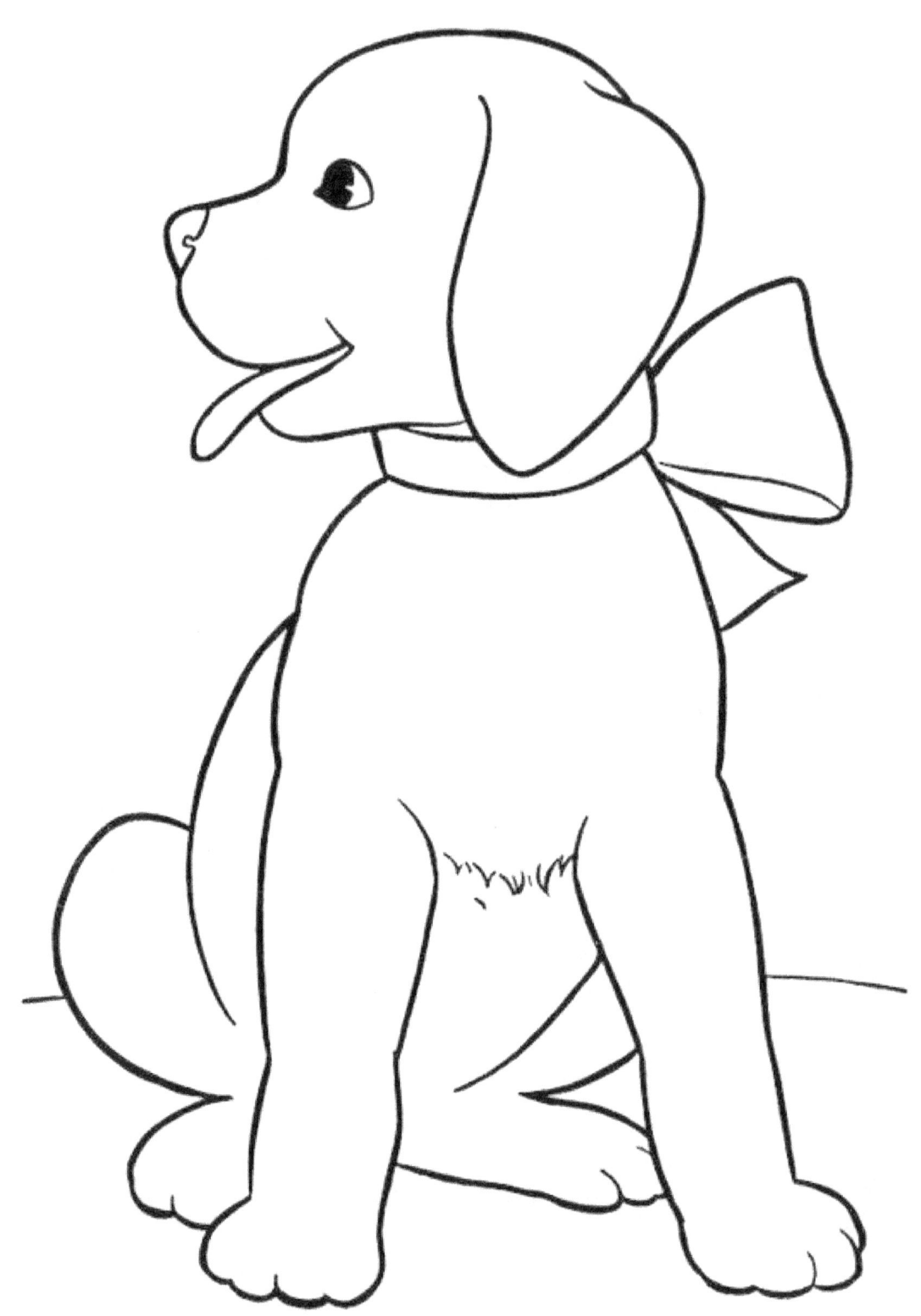

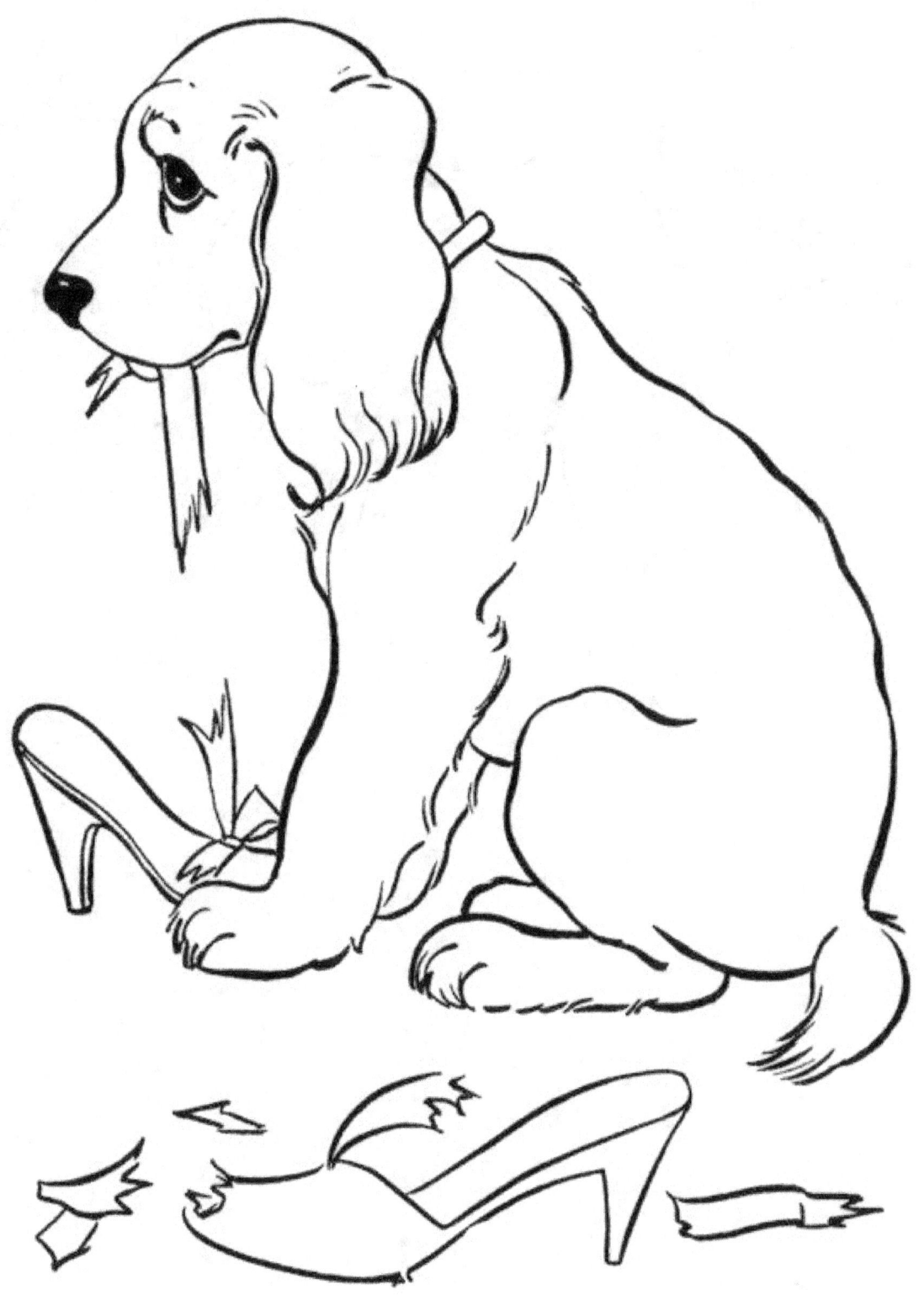

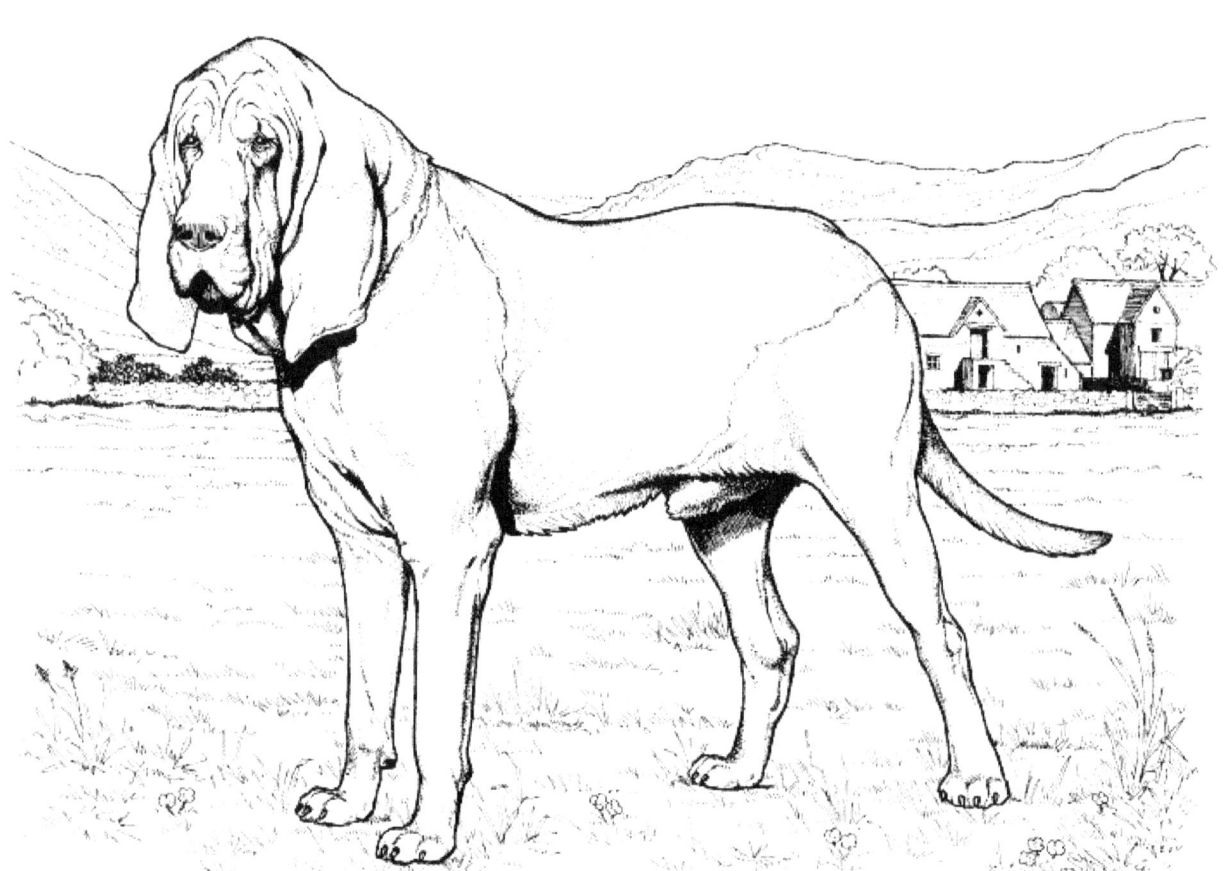

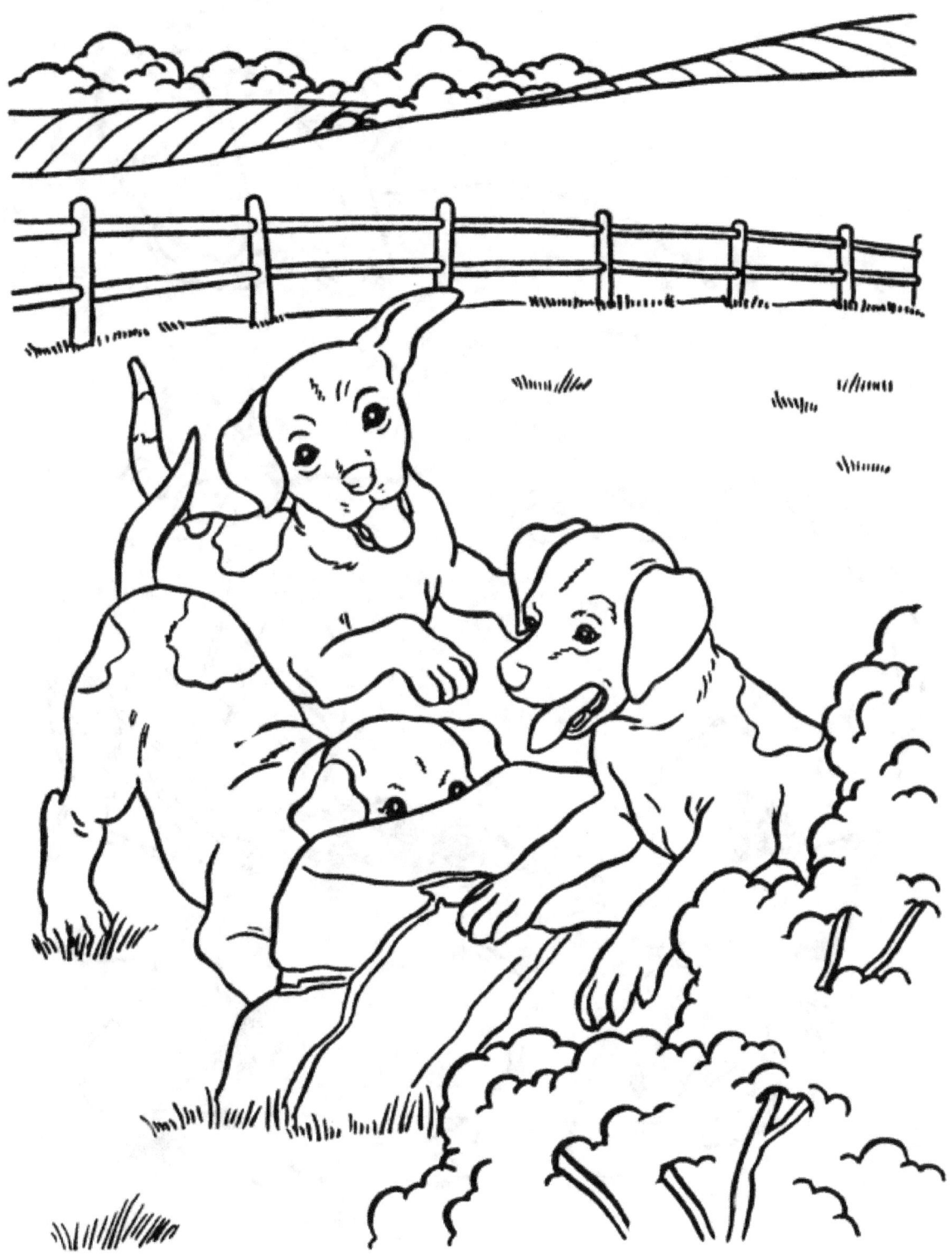

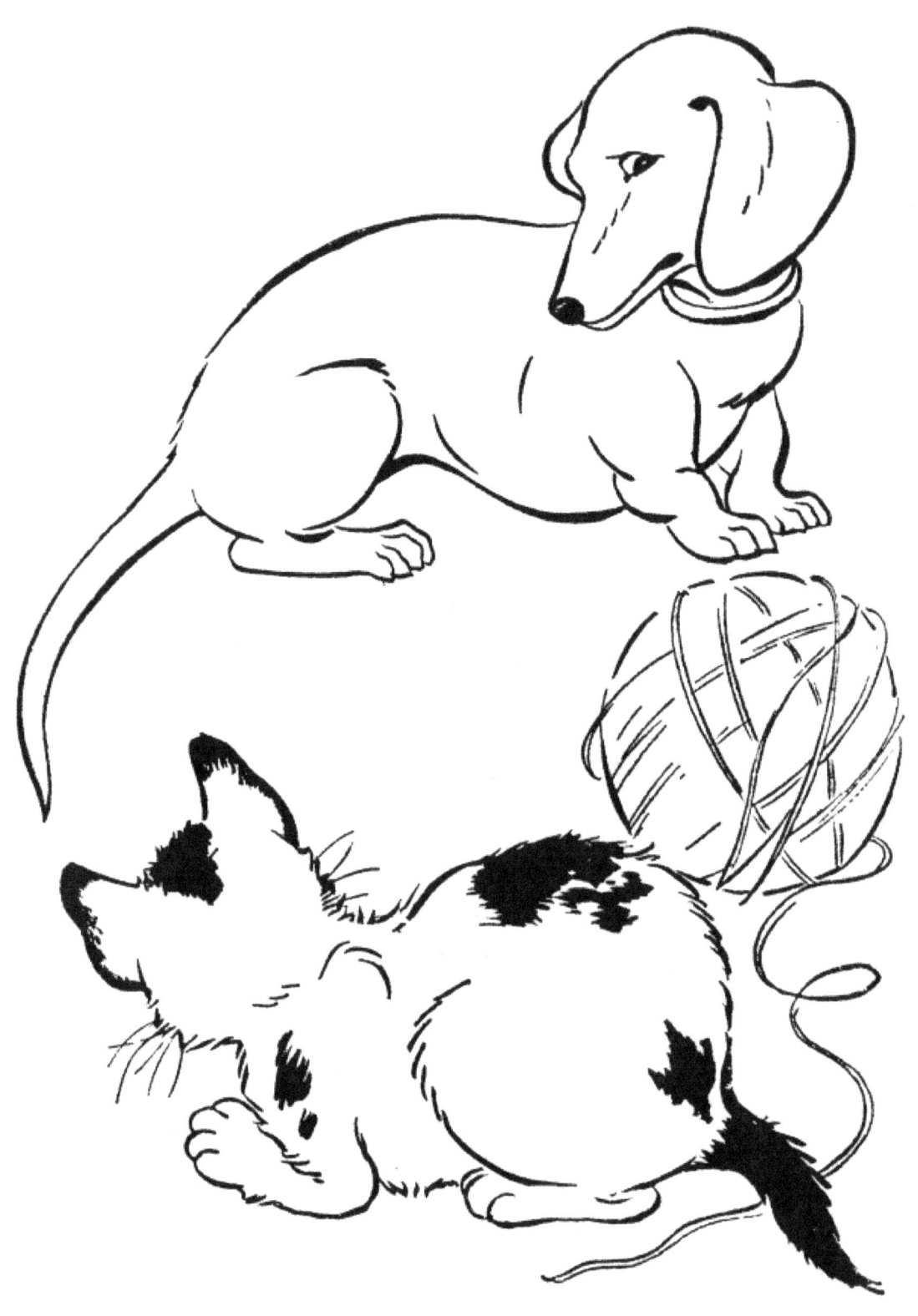

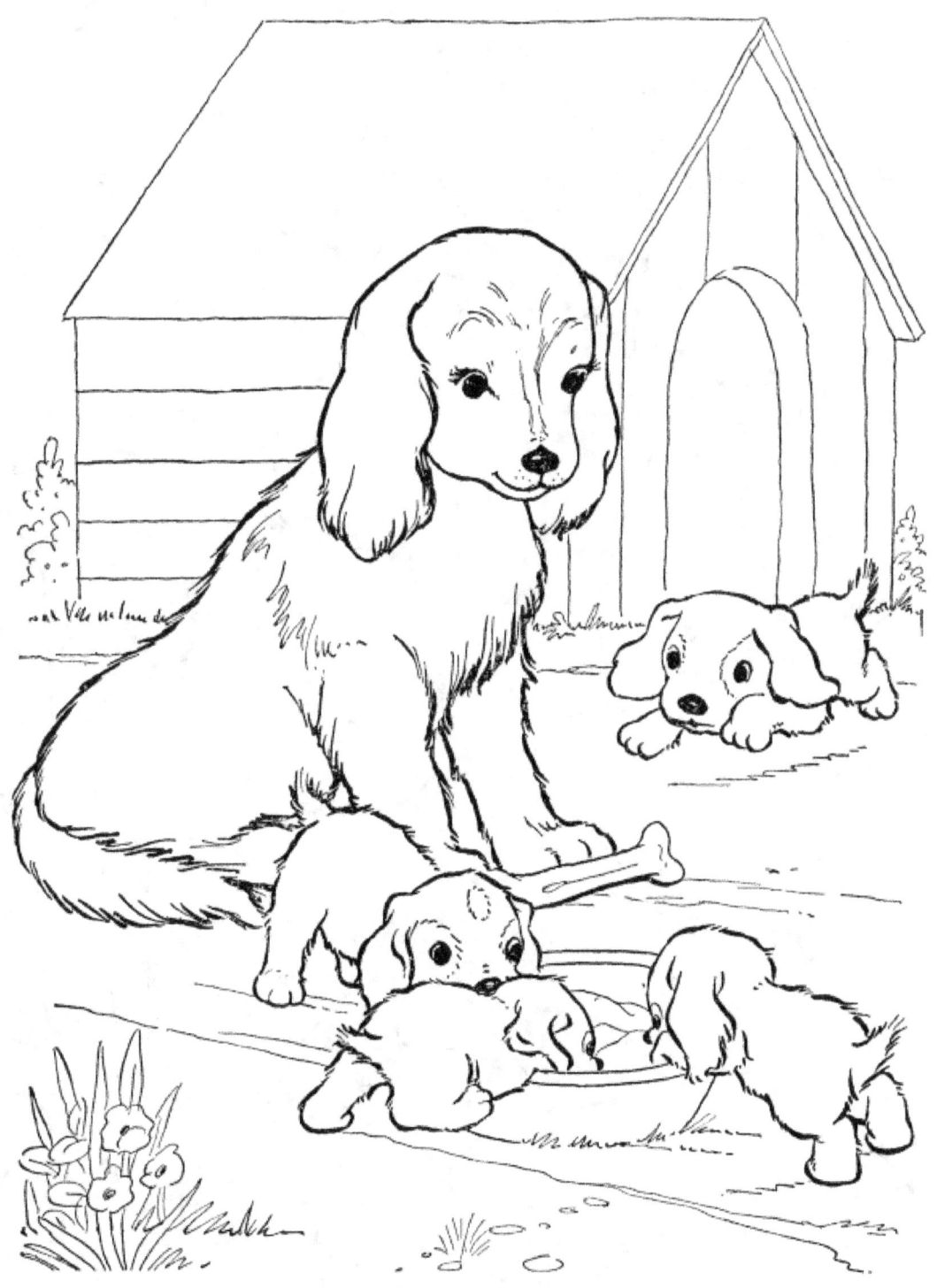

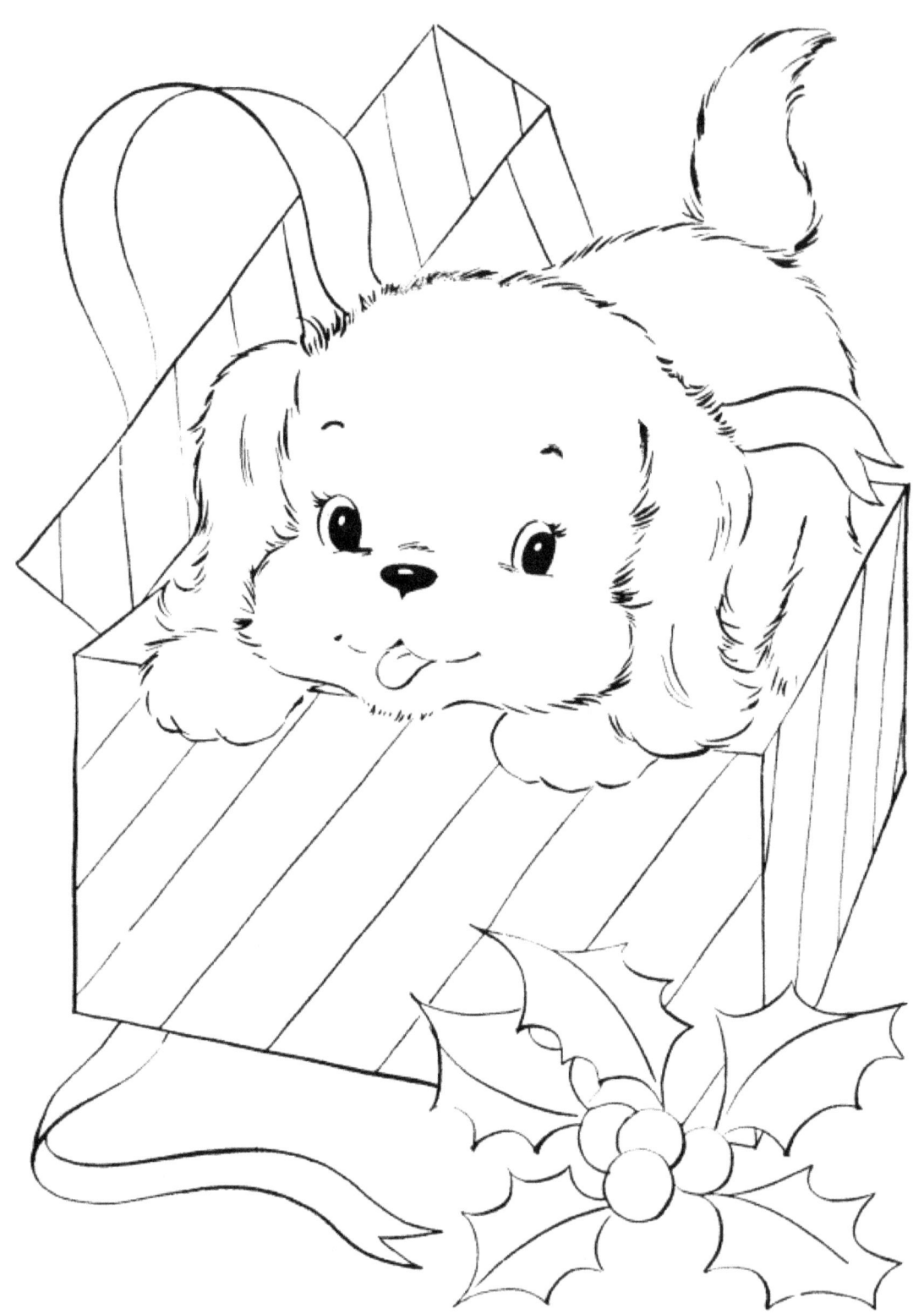

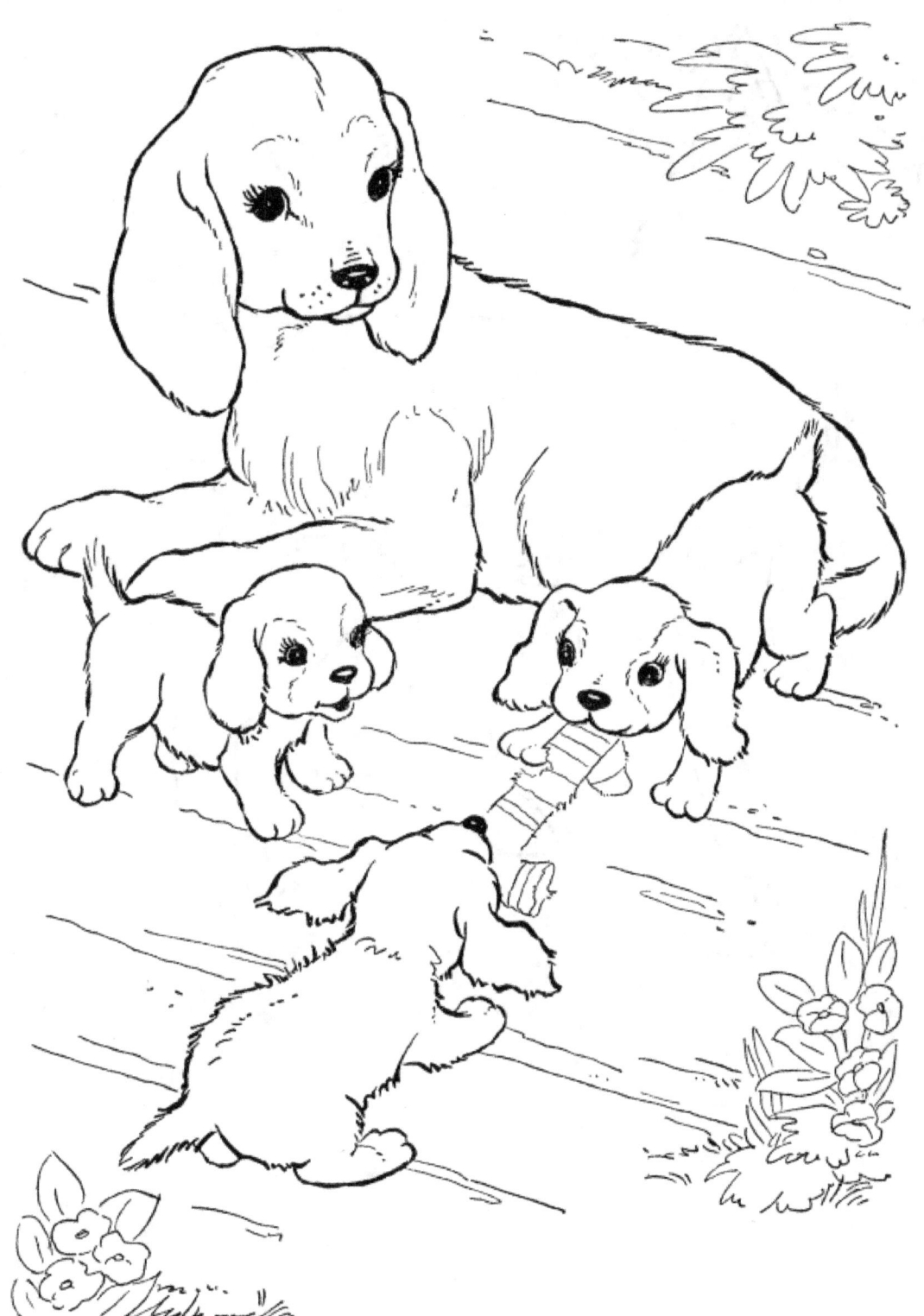

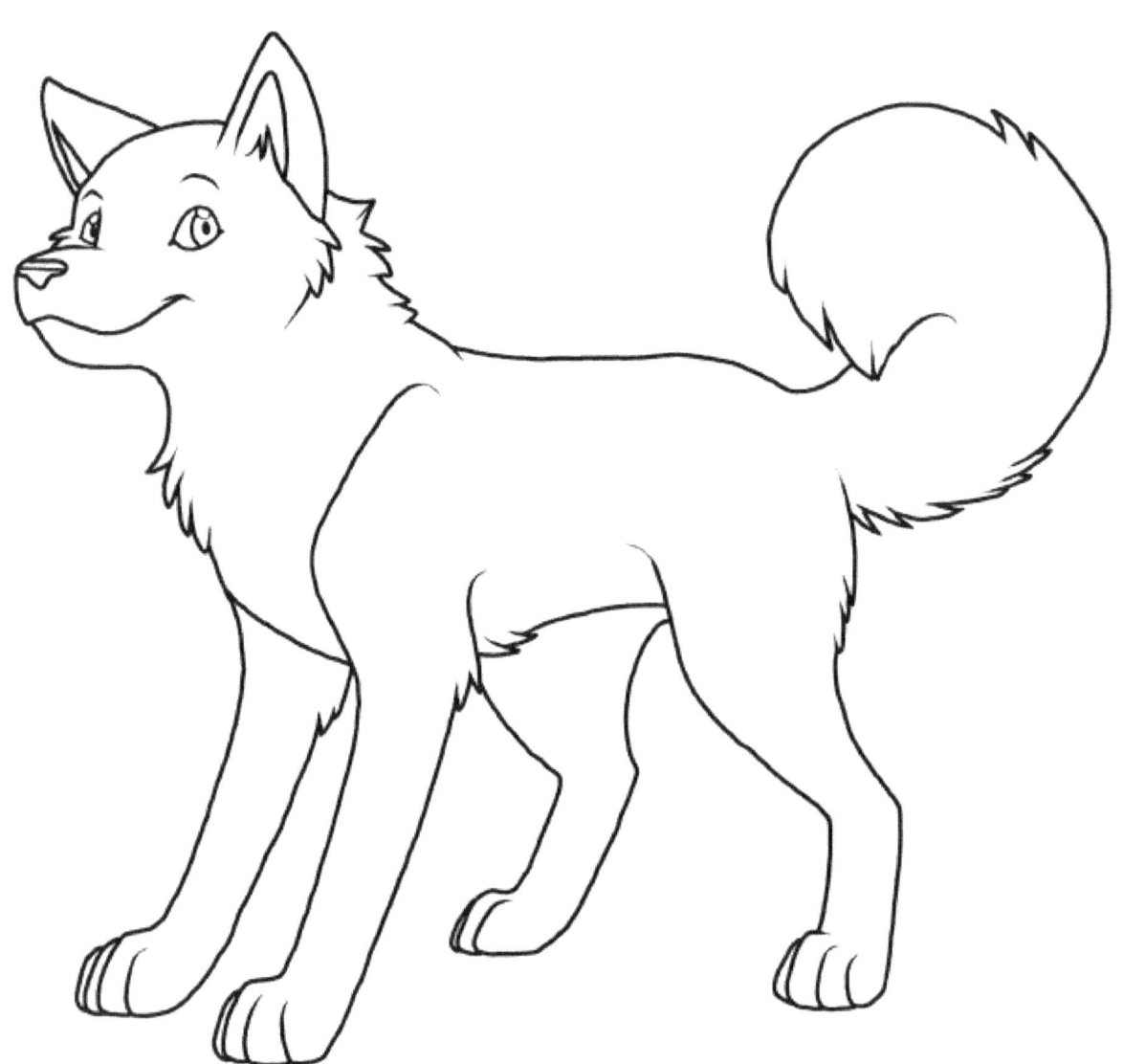

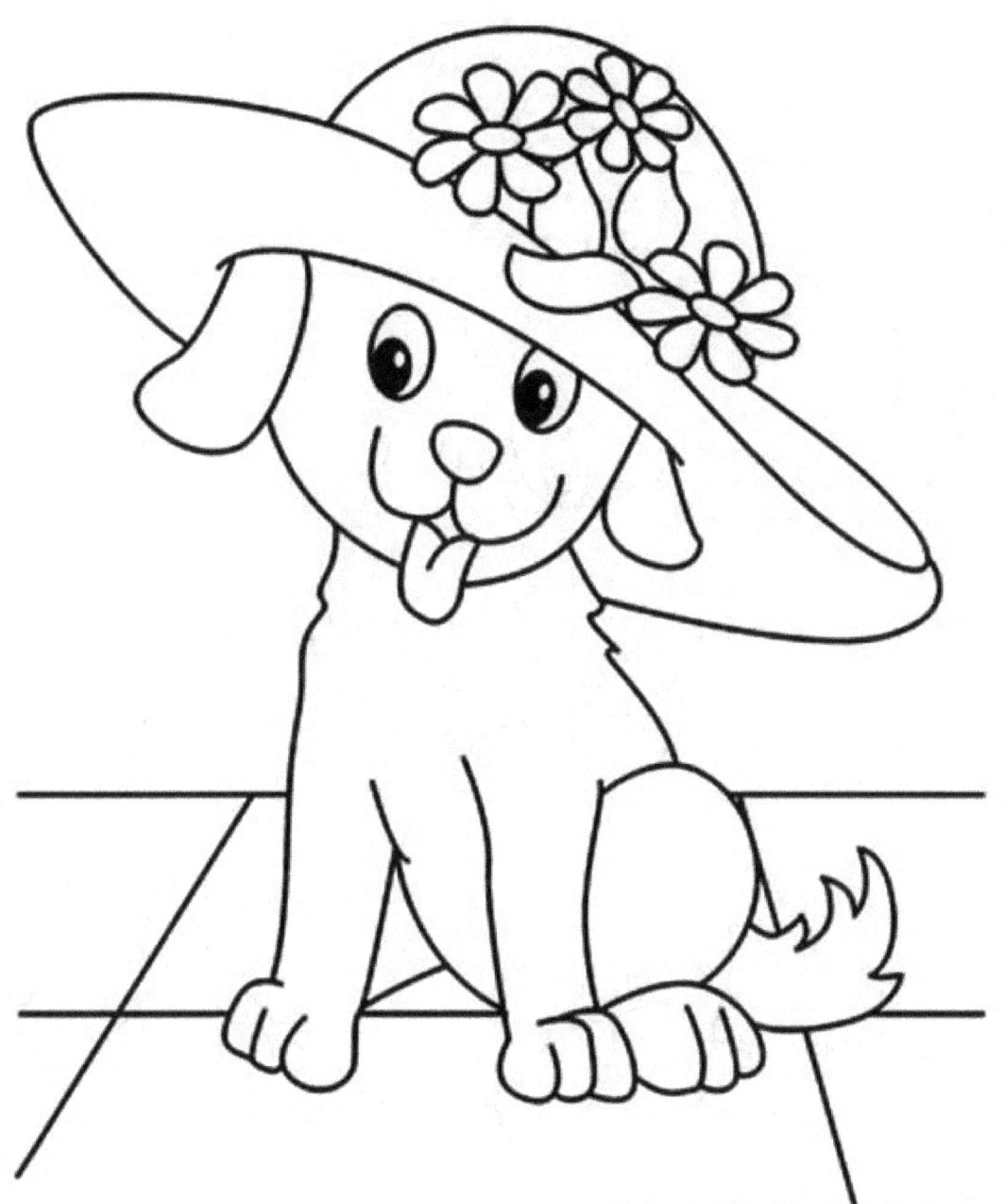

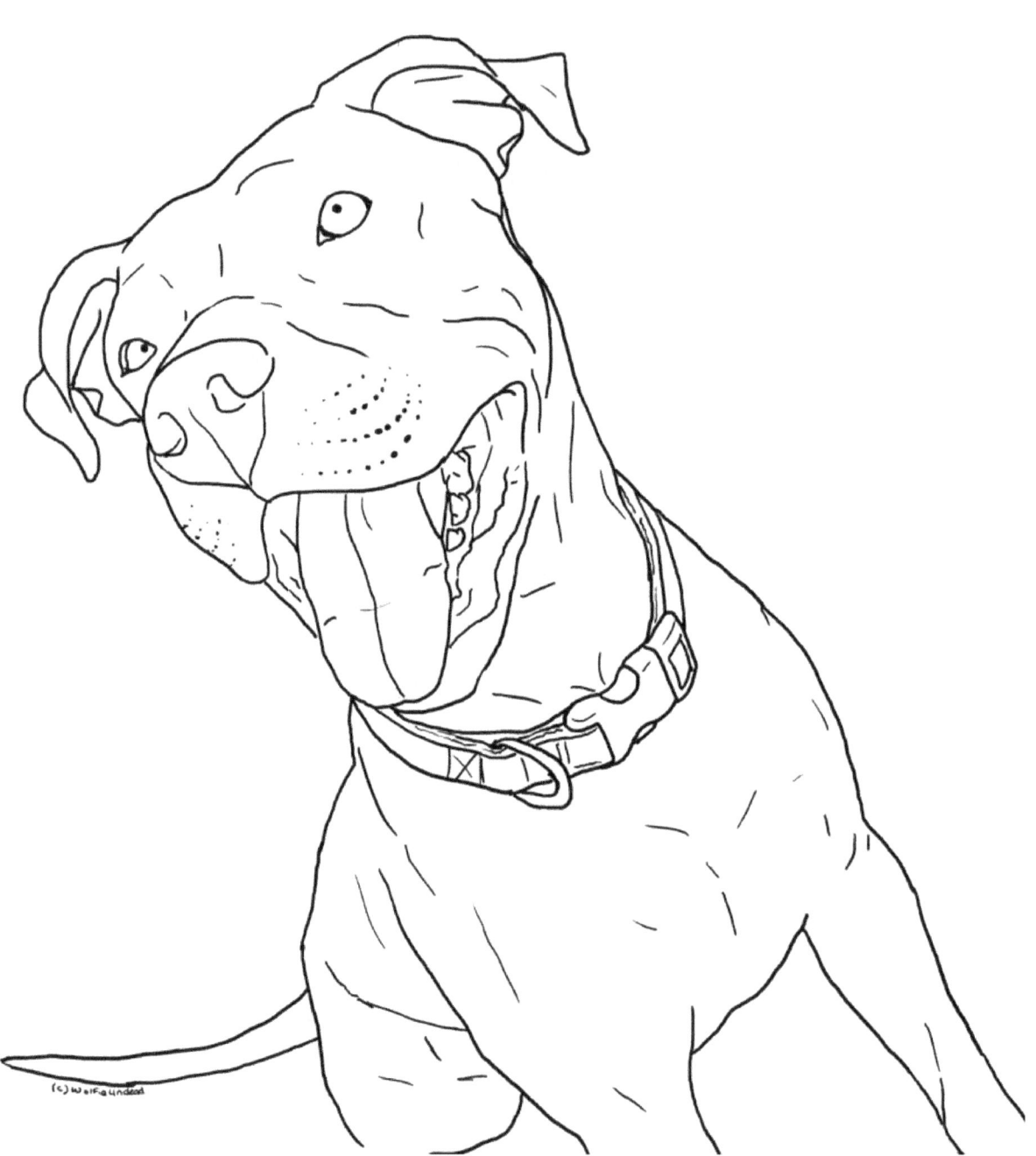

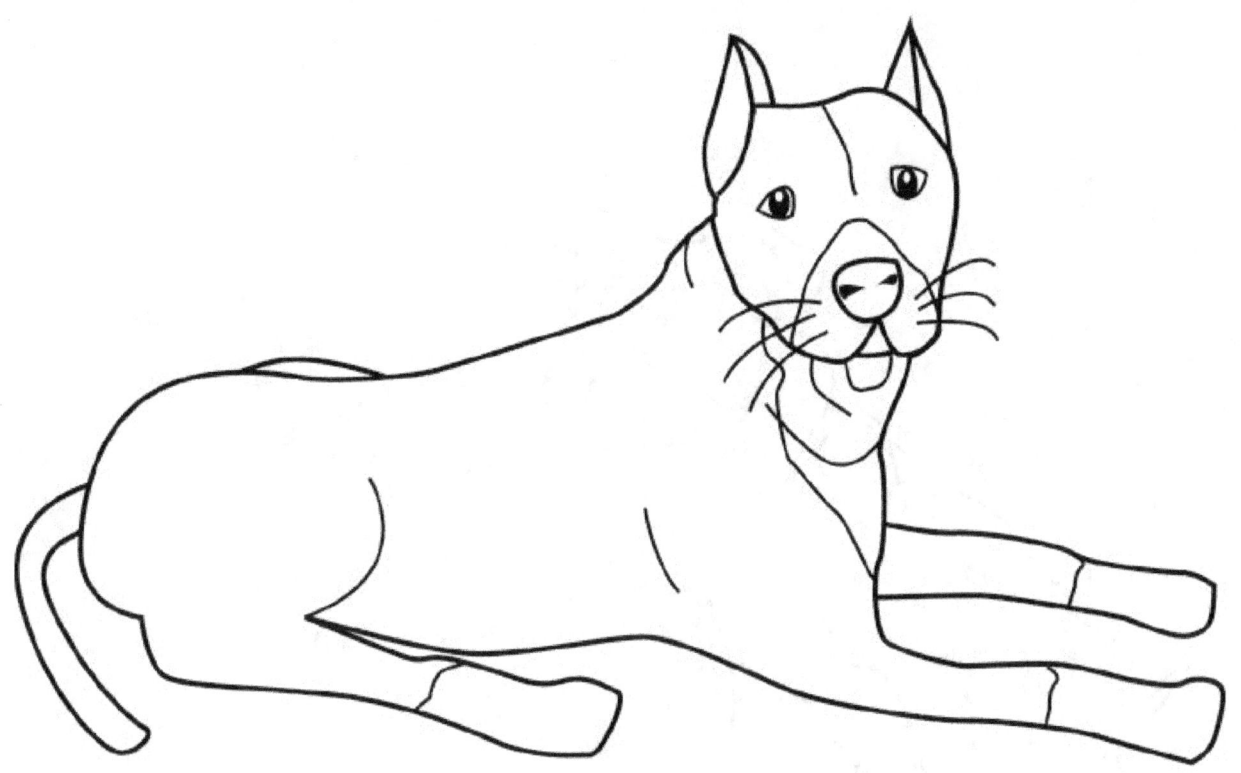

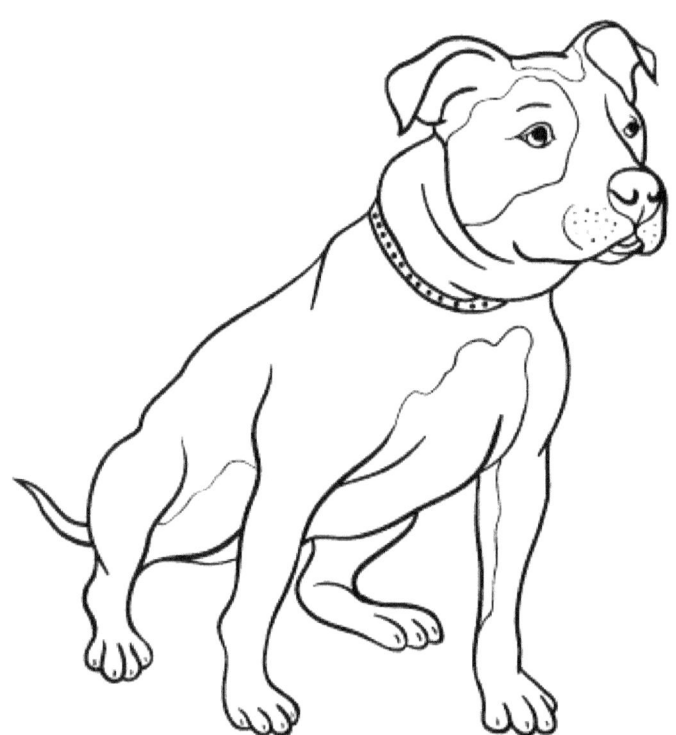